Minerals

by Patricia Brinkman

Table of Contents

Introduction 2
Chapter 1 What Are Minerals? 4
Chapter 2 What Are Minerals Like? 8
Chapter 3 Why Are Minerals Important? 12
Chapter 4 How Do People Use Minerals? 16
Summary 20
Glossary 22
Index 24

Introduction

Minerals are everywhere. Minerals are important to people. People use minerals for many things.

Read to learn about minerals.

Words to Know

 characteristics

 crust

 crystal

 gems

 metals

 minerals

 rocks

 solids

See the Glossary on page 22.

Chapter 1

What Are Minerals?

Minerals are **solids**. Minerals are natural. People do not make minerals.

▲ Quartz is a mineral. People do not make quartz.

Minerals are old. Minerals are in **rocks**. People get minerals from rocks.

▲ Some rocks have many minerals.

It's a Fact
Mining is taking minerals from rocks.

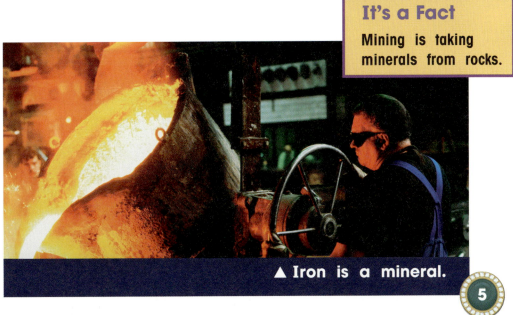
▲ Iron is a mineral.

Chapter 1

Minerals are in the ground. Minerals are not alive.

It's a Fact
A mineralogist is a scientist who studies minerals.

▲ **People get minerals from the ground.**

What Are Minerals?

Minerals are in many places. Food has minerals. The ocean has minerals. The **crust** of Earth has minerals.

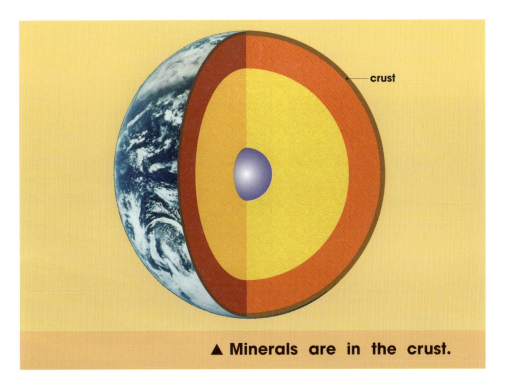

▲ Minerals are in the crust.

▲ Feldspar is a mineral. The crust of Earth has feldspar.

Chapter 2

What Are Minerals Like?

Minerals have different **characteristics**. Minerals have different colors. People name minerals because of color.

▲ Colors help people name minerals.

Each mineral has **crystal** patterns. Crystal patterns have shapes. People name minerals because of patterns.

Did You Know?
A crystal pattern is different shapes. A square is a crystal pattern. A rectangle is a crystal pattern.

▲ Quartz is a mineral. Quartz has this crystal pattern.

Chapter 2

Minerals feel different. Some minerals are hard. Hard minerals can scratch soft minerals.

▲ Diamonds are hard minerals.

Did You Know?

Talc is a soft mineral.
Talc is a powder.

What Are Minerals Like?

Some minerals are shiny.

▲ Pyrite is a shiny mineral.

▲ Gold is a shiny mineral.

All minerals break. Some minerals break with smooth sides. Some minerals break with sharp sides.

▲ This is a sharp side.

▲ This is a smooth side.

Chapter 3

Why Are Minerals Important?

Some minerals can keep people healthy. Some minerals are in food.

▲ Iron is a mineral. Spinach has iron.

Try This

Work with a partner.
1. Put cereal that has iron in a plastic bag.
2. Crush the cereal with your hand.
3. Hold a magnet over the cereal.
4. Tell what you see.

▲ Halite is a mineral.

Some minerals are **metals**. Many things have metals. Metals are important.

▲ What metals can you see?

Chapter 3

Some minerals burn to make energy. Energy is power. Energy is important.

▲ Coal is a mineral. People use coal to make energy.

Why Are Minerals Important?

Some countries sell minerals. These countries get money for minerals. These countries get minerals from the ground.

Did You Know?
Some countries do not have many minerals.

▲ Gold is a mineral. Countries get gold from the ground.

Chapter 4

How Do People Use Minerals?

People use minerals in many ways. People use metals in many things. People use metals every day.

▲ People use metals.

People use minerals to make energy. People use energy to make light. People use energy to heat homes.

▲ People use energy.

Chapter 4

People use minerals every day. People use minerals in pencils. People use minerals in toothpaste. People use minerals on farms.

Did You Know?
People found 3,000 types of minerals.

▲ People use minerals in many ways.

How Do People Use Minerals?

People use minerals for jewelry. Some minerals are **gems**. Gems are difficult to find.

▲ A diamond is a gem.

▲ A ruby is a gem.

▲ An emerald is a gem.

Summary

People need minerals. Minerals come from the ground. People use minerals in many ways. Minerals are important.

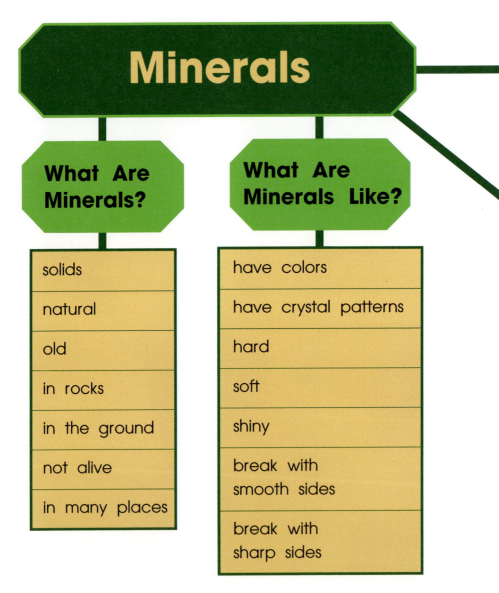

Why Are Minerals Important?	keep people healthy
	metals
	energy
	money

How Do People Use Minerals?	metals to make things
	to make energy
	in pencils
	in toothpaste
	on farms
	for jewelry

Think About It

1. What are some characteristics of minerals?
2. Tell three reasons minerals are important.
3. Make a list of minerals you use.

Glossary

characteristics features that help describe something

Minerals have different **characteristics**.

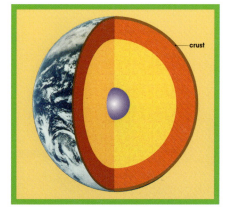

crust the top layer of Earth

The **crust** of Earth has minerals.

crystal the regular shape minerals take

Each mineral has **crystal** patterns.

gems beautiful, rare minerals

Some minerals are **gems**.

metals minerals that conduct energy

Some minerals are **metals**.

minerals solid natural materials of many colors and types

Minerals are natural.

rocks solid parts of the crust of Earth

Minerals are in **rocks**.

solids matter that has shape

Minerals are **solids**.

Index

characteristics, 8

colors, 8

crust, 7

crystal, 9

energy, 14, 17

food, 7, 12

gems, 19

hard, 10

light, 17

metals, 13, 16

minerals, 2–20

natural, 4

ocean, 7

old, 5

rocks, 5

shiny, 11

soft, 10

solids, 4